MARKETING
BLUEPRINT
FOR
CONTRACTORS

The *Fastest* and Easiest Ways
to
DOUBLE YOUR PROFITS
in
90 Days or LESS!

By: Tony Bernard

MarketingBlueprintForContractors.com

ISBN-13: 978-1517237271
ISBN-10: 1517237270

Disclaimer

The author and publisher of this and any accompanying resources and or materials have used their best efforts in preparing them. The author and publisher make no representation or warranties with respect to the accuracy, applicability, fitness, or completeness of the contents. **The information contained here is strictly for educational and informational purposes ONLY.**

Therefore, if you wish to apply ideas contained, you take full responsibility for your actions.

The author and publisher of this book disclaim any warranties (express or implied), merchantability, or fitness of materials expressed for any particular purpose. The author and publisher shall in no event be held liable to any party for any direct, indirect, punitive, special, incidental or other consequential damages arising directly or indirectly from any use of this material, which is provided as is, and without warranties.

As always, the advice of a competent legal, tax, accounting or other applicable professional should be sought before using any materials found here or elsewhere.

The author and publisher do not warrant the performance, effectiveness or applicability of any sites listed or linked to in this book.

All links are for information purposes only and are not warranted for content, accuracy or any other implied or explicit purpose.

CONTACT INFORMATION:

Support@MarketingBlueprintForContractors.com

DEDICATION

This book is dedicated to my wife and children who have shown me love and support in all I do and to God for putting them in my life.

TABLE OF CONTENTS

Tony Bernard

ACKNOWLEDGEMENTS

First and foremost I would like to thank God for the gifts, talents, abilities and experiences that He has provided me and people that He has put into my life.

To my parents, Aunt Germain, Uncle Leo and others who have nurtured me and helped me make better decisions.

To my wife, Kelley and our daughters, Kaitlyn and Maeghan. I thank God for you. You are the best things about my life! You gave me something to work for. Contributing to others and a better life for us is what I want. This book is part of that!

FORWARD

BY: DAVE LEAVITT

I have worked in the Construction Profession for over 40 years. During that time, I have had both the privilege and pleasure to meet, get to know, work with, and learn from more than a thousand skilled Construction Management Professionals. These were leaders who could transform diverse individuals into High Performance Teams, and help them achieve great accomplishments by focusing their talents. These people were catalysts for Continuous Improvement. These are some of the gifted Professionals who drive our Industry.

In that same time, I have also worked with perhaps 30 - 40 Marketing Professionals who helped sell those same Construction Skills. These professionals were able to succinctly communicate how their companies were different from the competition and what was their unique selling proposition (USP). These folks helped sell Construction Services and close countless contracts in very competitive, increasingly globalized markets.

In all those years I have only known one individual who had truly mastered both those skill sets. Tony Bernard is that person. I have worked with Tony on 5 different projects over a span of 20 years and he has consistently demonstrated an in-depth mastery of both The Construction Profession and Marketing Professions. During these last 20 years, I have come to know Tony on both a personal and professional level, and **I can say without qualification that he is the consummate Construction Professional.** Tony has played a critical role in the success realized on each project he was involved with. **Tony has a unique skills set that combines both**

Construction and Marketing expertise that is truly rare in the industry. Tony has honed these skills through decades of hands on experience with over 60 different clients and in excess of $15 Billion worth of projects, always with proven results. He has consistently demonstrated an in-depth knowledge of, and a mastery of, Best Practices in both the marketing and construction fields.

Tony's easy going style of "Socratic Questioning" always seems to pull the best out of everyone on the team. He methodically pursues and follows up until he has identified the critical issues on any topic. For years, I have enjoyed Tony's corollaries Of SAQ (should ask questions) to the standard FAQ's. There are many in our Industry with lots of knowledge, but far fewer who have the wisdom to properly apply it. **I have always considered us truly blessed when we could engage Tony on another challenging proposal or project.**

When I learned that Tony was compiling his decades of experiences, lessons learned and best practices into a tool that was custom tailored to help those in the profession, I was thrilled. Here is an opportunity to capture decades of practical experience, best practices, lessons learned and, insight in a succinct, comparatively brief package, to better your outcome. Our Profession needs more innovation and more communication of best practices. Our profession needs more leaders working for continuous improvement.

I can recommend Tony Bernard, without qualification, to any Business Professional seeking to better their situation, differentiate themselves or who truly embrace Continuous Improvement. I hope you will take the time to reach out to Tony, get to know him and get his perspective and insights on your business.

I will close with a final thought: some of you may be wondering why do this? I can guess that those who are asking this question don't yet know Tony. Those who do know Tony, understand that he truly enjoys helping others. He is both a lifelong student and lifelong teacher. Those of us who know Tony personally, know that he is a man of Faith. He believes that we all have a responsibility to better ourselves and help each other, so I will end this with one of his favorite Quotations: "As iron sharpens iron, so one man sharpens another." Proverbs 27 : 17

Dave Leavitt, August 2015

TESTIMONIALS

*"Tony hits it right on the head again. **Marketing Blueprint for Contractors** is a must for any contractor who wants to make more money by standing out from the contractor crowd. Tony lays out 6 pillars that can be implemented immediately. When you do this, your marketing instantly becomes more effective and your prospects will recognize that you are the contractor to trust and do business with."*

Leon Hatzenbihler
Fine Point Marketing,
FinePointMarketing.com

# # #

*"I'm a professional marketer always looking to improve my craft, and **I have to say, it was relieving and exciting to find a book that concisely and strategically focuses on high-leverage activities.** It isn't just an array of tactics in this book -- **it is foundational strategies.** They are elements I will use both with my own business and for others I work with. **I highly recommend the book, specifically on the chapters on SAQs and the section on Ad Writing. GOLD!"***

David J. Bradley, MBA
Managing Director, **Primal Digital Marketing - primaldm.com**

# # #

"In Marketing Blueprint For Contractors, Tony has masterfully done what many people have often failed to do. He has combined his extensive experience working on over $15 Billion in local & international construction projects with his strategic and practical marketing approach and his unwavering desire to help those in need.

Tony truly understands, better than anyone, that knowing your craft and selling your craft are two different things. He helps you bridge the gap between them both by the ideas, strategies, and executable items outlined in Marketing Blueprint For Contractors.

Ever since I met Tony at a marketing training seminar in San Diego, California, back in 2010, he has always been a straight shooter, filled with knowledge and insight, and an all-around great guy. I'm proud to call him my friend."

Joe Valmonte, Publisher & Founder of MODERN ENTREPRENEUR www.JoeValmonte.com

# # #

"Tony Bernard is a good friend and colleague. We are both Certified Power Marketing Consultants so he gave me an opportunity to read a prerelease copy of his new book and I want you to know how blessed you are to have his **'Marketing Blueprint for Contractors'** book. Tony has revealed the foundational principles that make our marketing work so effectively across so many businesses. All you have to do is apply them. **There is money and power in this book. Use it wisely.**"

Terry Brandon
www.Marketing-Dominator.com

# # #

"Tony Bernard's new book is an eye-opener for any contractor. You can say, 'So what? Information is everywhere today.' But here's the truth — Tony provides insights, not just info.

If you google a contractor in your local area, you'll see a bunch of results, including yourself and your competitors. If you put yourself in your prospect's shoes, whom would you hire, honestly?

The truth is, you'd have trouble choosing one contractor over another. And Tony explains exactly why this happens and what to do about it, because not

Tony Bernard

knowing this is killing your revenue. And this is NOT a book on internet marketing techniques - those are dime a dozen.

What he gives you is a whole array of strategies and tactics that you can implement today, even if you stay away from the internet at all, if you choose to.

Everything here is applicable to both online and offline marketing. Most importantly, it's about results. As a Certified Power Marketing Consultant, Tony's goal is to have you double your business in less than a year, and he has the chops to back it up.

In summary, great book. And very readable, too. Buy it but, most importantly, use it."

Philip Saparov - E-Learning Professional
www.TutorPhil.com

# # #

"I want to thank you for allowing me to use your insights on the power of following up with future customers.

When I shared what you teach at my recent seminar here in New Zealand the crowd looked like the scales had fallen from their eyes. **By implementing this one simple tactic that you teach, any business can significantly increase its revenues at a very low initial cost.**

Thank you for sharing this valuable insight."

Mike Noone - Business growth and Innovation Consultant
TippingPointMarketing.co

# # #

"Tony, I wanted so say as long as I've known you, I've been drawn to and inspired by your intelligence, integrity, and family values. You have an undeniable thirst for learning and staying current to provide the best service to your clients and **'Marketing Blueprint for Contractors'** is no exception. You have transformational strategies throughout the chapters and your clients will benefit *greatly without a doubt once they hire you to help them implement these strategies. Way to stay on the cutting edge and congratulations on the new book. :)"*

~Mario Fachini - 2x #1 Best Selling Author & Speaker
www.MarioFachini.com

# # #

"I congratulate my friend, Tony Bernard, on his book – 'Marketing Blueprint for Contractors'. I have known Tony for over 20 years, both in business and as a friend.

Tony has always carried himself as a gentleman of character, integrity and honesty, so I am assured that 'Marketing Blueprint for Contractors' portrays those same traits. Tony's loving dedication to his family is carried over to his business associations. When you become involved with Tony, you become "family".

Tony has the personality of sensing when and where someone needs help and is always there with a helping hand - a helping hand of generosity beyond the call of duty. His giving character serves him well and shines brightly on him.

In 'Marketing Blueprint for Contractors', Tony brings forth in written form the same highly successful practices he has exercised and implemented for the many years he has assisted contractors and the construction industry. His dedicated methodology for expediting projects to optimum cost effective fruition and optimum profits surely creates a proprietary reason for wanting to make his methodology available to a broader arena of contractors and construction projects. 'Marketing Blueprint for Contractors' provides the vehicle to that purpose. Maybe the title should be 'Tony's Helping Hand for Contractors' because 'Marketing Blueprint for Contractors' is truly an extension of Tony's generous and willing helping hand.

Glen Bartholomew - Diversified Financial Services
Author of *"Growing Up Is ... !!!"* - NOT Just For Kids
www.GrowingUpIs.com

# # #

Chapter 1

Introduction

Dear Friend,

Welcome to Marketing Blueprint For Contractors the Book!

This represents nearly 25 years of hard work, study and research.

I wanted to share some thoughts with you in no particular order about what to expect in this book.

First - There are lots of opportunities for you to go deeper in this wonderful area of your business … Marketing! I would love to work with you if you are open minded and wanting more success!

Second - This book was put together in a short period of time and I'm not striving for perfection. That is really never reached and it cost you way too much time.

Many people want to write a book. They talk about it, some even start it, but very few finish it. I feel blessed to have actually finished this book!

This is my first book and there are probably some errors in it, I would really appreciate it if you would just email me about any mistakes.

Tony@MarketingBlueprintForContractorsBook.com

Please include the page and the item that needs correction. Thank you in advance for your help and time!

Third - This book is intended to help you grow your business. It is not a novel or written by some English teacher. It is a short concise book, not full of fluff!

Fourth – This book is for implementers. You'll see there's **lots** of ideas that you can use to grow your business or DOUBLE Your Profits!

Finally – If you don't like the book, I'm ok with that. I'll refund your cost, if it is a Kindle or paperback! I don't want any unhappy readers! Just forward your Amazon receipt to my email address and you'll get your refund from me personally.

Tony@MarketingBlueprintForContractorsBook.com

Please don't leave a negative review because you found a spelling, grammar error broken link. Life's too short for whiners and complainers! We can part as friends and leave it that way and I'll refund you your investment.

Having said that, if you like what you read, or most of what you read, I'd love to hear from you and get to know you better and find out what you learned. Apply for the Free 30 Minute Consultation after you have read this book.

MarketingBlueprintForContractors.com/Consultation

To your success!

Tony Bernard
Winslow, Maine – USA

P.S. **Read this book, but more importantly, implement at least one of these Profit Multipliers and you will see significant improvements in your profits!**

Tony Bernard

P.P.S. See if you qualify for the Free Consultation, because I'll answer any questions and help get you clear on what is the best steps forward are for your specific situation!

MarketingBlueprintForContractors.com/Consultation

This book is based on the Video Presentation at

MarketingBlueprintForContractorsBook.com/Presentation

The presentation is updated from time to time because we want to provide you the latest information.

MarketingBlueprintForContractors.com

CHAPTER 2

WHO IS TONY BERNARD

"Doing what you have always done in Marketing,
will get you what you have always gotten.
NOW is the time to DOUBLE YOUR PROFITS!"

Tony Bernard

I'm an Amazon #1 Best Selling Author, Speaker and International Consultant. I became a "Certified Power Marketing Consultant" in May 2013. Plus I have had the good fortune to have worked in the construction industry for over 35 years on over $15 Billion worth of projects so far in my career.

Let me give you a little more history.

I started in the construction industry full time in 1980 after college and had a great run until the company I was working for started going through difficult times and ultimately I was laid off in 1991. I tried to find work locally but the companies willing to hire me would have me working away from my family for months at a time.

I looked into starting my own Construction Consulting business but this was proving to be a difficult task. I had technical skills, but few Marketing skills. As I started to learn Marketing I could see the leverage Marketing could provide so I became a student of Marketing. I started investing time and effort into Marketing Programs, Courses, Seminars, Workshops etc. to help get my Consulting business get off the ground.

My Consulting business ended up doing well, but work would still require me to travel sometimes for weeks at a time, causing me to be away from my family (wife and daughters).

Things started to get critical for me as I needed to make a decision on where I wanted to take my life. I needed to decide if I wanted to stay in the Construction Consulting business or if I wanted to move into the Marketing for Contractors niche: something I felt very confident and comfortable doing from all the knowledge I have gained and learned over the years.

It would be great for me to have better control of my income and work location. Like going to the faucet and turning on the water when you want some. So, that is what I did. I decided to help contractors with Marketing. Now I have a faucet to turn on and get as much money as I want, when I want. And this book will help you do the same in your business!

I decided to study actual proven masters in Marketing. They had to have proven track records in building their own business and other businesses - not just talk the talk. But walk the talk. Practice what they preach in other words!

So, I decided to commit to helping contractors with Marketing! I started attending private and exclusive events such as Mastermind groups, Summits, Retreats and Workshops that took me all across the US, attending these live events.

Over my 24 years as a Consultant I've accumulated significant amounts of experience, knowledge, strategies and techniques; not to mention a huge library of marketing books written by the top gurus in the industry from past to present, thousands of documents and PDFs and thousands of videos all containing extremely valuable information pertaining to Marketing.

Some of these events had price tags of $5,000, $10,000, $15,000, $25,000 or more.

I conservatively estimate my marketing library to be valued at over $255,000.

I'm also a member of several high end Mastermind groups! If you have ever joined one, you'll know how much they are worth! Sometimes one small item from one meeting can be worth tens of thousands of dollars or much, much more when implemented of course!

This book is based on the Video Presentation at

MarketingBlueprintForContractorsBook.com/Presentation

The presentation is updated from time to time because we want to provide you the latest information.

Chapter 3

Introduction to Marketing

"I can always fix my problems with better marketing!"

Gary Halbert

Marketing is your greatest leverage tool! Where else can you get 10, 20, 50, 100, or 200% returns or even higher? Often times with some minor changes to current ads, website or Marketing Materials!

Do I Have your Attention? I hope so!

What you will learn here will change your thinking about Marketing. It will increase your profits … if you implement any of these ideas!

Here's What You'll Learn

- Why your current Marketing costs you money when it should make you money.

- **Totally New Marketing Perspective.**

- Discover 6 Easy ways to quickly double your profits.

- **Also two case studies**.

- Why This Is Important **To You NOW!**

- Most of the advertising you are currently doing is not providing you with the results **you deserve for YOUR hard work!**

- **I'll explain why it is NOT your fault and you'll totally understand once you read it.**

- Learn what type of marketing you should be using to get an actual positive rate of return on investment (ROI).

Is This For You?

- Are you open minded?

- **If you want more business, this is for you!**

- If you want more profits, this is for you!

- **If you want to be able to pick and choose your jobs.**

- If you're worried about the economy because of the impending market correction.

And Finally …

This is for YOU because you're going to discover Simple Sound Marketing principles so **YOU can thrive no matter what!**

Bottom Line, so you can have FREEDOM and CERTAINTY about YOUR business!

Okay, let's get started, but I have a few **House Rules**

- Not for Get Rich Quick people.

- **Not for "Dabblers"** (Serious People ONLY!)

- For Action Takers ONLY.

One last thing about any Results mentioned in this book.

Any results mentioned here are NOT typical! Most people who buy any "How to build their business" training will not make any money whatsoever, because they don't apply the information.

"Damaging admission of fact", but this is well known but nobody has the guts to say it.

Let me introduce you to … the 6 Profit Multipliers!

The *Fastest* and Easiest Ways to DOUBLE YOUR Profits in 90 Days or LESS!

This book is based on the Video Presentation at

MarketingBlueprintForContractorsBook.com/Presentation

The presentation is updated from time to time because we want to provide you the latest information.

CHAPTER 4

INTRODUCTION TO THE 6 PROFIT MULTIPLIERS

"If you want something you've never had, you must be willing to do something you've never done."

Thomas Jefferson

Here is the list of the 6 Profit Multipliers

1. Marketing Mindset

2. Unique Selling Proposition (USP)

3. Follow Up

4. Strategic Messaging Formula (SMS)

5. Frequently Asked Questions (FAQ)

6. Should Ask Questions (SAQ)

Now let's talk more about each profit multiplier.

This book is based on the Video Presentation at

MarketingBlueprintForContractorsBook.com/Presentation

The presentation is updated from time to time because we want to provide you the latest information.

MarketingBlueprintForContractors.com

CHAPTER 5

PROFIT MULTIPLIER 1

MARKETING MINDSET

*"You are the average of the 5 people
you spend the most time with."*

Jim Rohn

First let's start with the correct mindset! To be specific, the proper Marketing Mindset that is.

Let's address 3 main items that are currently killing your marketing!

- Fragmented Marketing.

- **Use of Platitudes.**

- Plus, you are using the **wrong Type of Marketing**.

Fragmented Marketing

This is not having a comprehensive or consistent messaging, plan or strategy for your marketing or advertising! The basic framework is missing for these across ALL Channels – Website, Radio, TV, Display Ads (newspaper, trade journals), Videos, etc.

Who are YOU listening to for your marketing advice?

Who has your best interest at heart?

The Yellow Page Sales Person?

The Newspaper Sales Person?

The Radio Sales Person?

The Website Sales Person?

The SEO Sales Person?

And the worst thing about this ... They ALL think they are "Marketing Consultants"! This is helping to create your "Fragmented Marketing".

Next is .... Platitudes

The Use of Platitudes is not allowing you to stand out or above your competition.

Let me define Platitudes: words & phrases that are devoid of any real meaning. A statement that expresses an idea that is not new.

Examples of Platitudes:

- Gets the job done right the first time

- **X years of service**

- Largest selection

- **Highest quality**

- Best service

- **Number one**

- State of the Art

- **Honest**

- Professional

- **Largest Selection**

- Biggest in the State

- **Family Owned**

- Most Reliable

- **In Business Since 1900**

- Lowest Prices *(Please don't go for this one. You would be shooting yourself not in the foot but in the head!)*

How many of these are in your ads? **Now be honest!** How many of these meaningless words are in your marketing materials and ads?

Pick up the Yellow Pages and look at the display ads for your industry! They all pretty much say the same meaningless things (Platitudes)!

Think about any of your ads, advertising, or marketing materials. How many of these platitude statements are in your ads?

Finally, lets' talk about the Two Basic Ad Types

1. **Institutional Advertising**
   Institutional advertising is just getting their name out there.

   Example: *Pepsi, General Electric, General Motors.*

2. **Menu Board Style Advertising**
   Here is what we offer:

   > Good, Better, Best;
   > Bronze, Silver, Gold.

   Example: fast food restaurants, *Wendy's, McDonalds, etc.*

Which one do you use most? 1 or 2?

Be honest!

Going forward, I have a BETTER Ad Type that I want you to use!

It is called …… "Direct Response Advertising!"

Direct Response Advertising is where we want Prospects to take some specific action after watching, listening to or reading your information (Ad or marketing materials).

Some examples may be to call you, download a free report, get a coupon, etc.

That is why it is called "Direct Response". **This is HUGE! You'll learn more about this in the chapter about "Strategic Messaging Formula" (Chapter 8)!**

This book is based on the Video Presentation at

MarketingBlueprintForContractorsBook.com/Presentation

The presentation is updated from time to time because we want to provide you the latest information.

CHAPTER 6

PROFIT MULTIPLIER 2

UNIQUE SELLING PROPOSITION (USP)

"Make it simple. Make it memorable. Make it inviting to look at. Make it fun to read."

Leo Burnett

USP stands for **U**nique **S**elling **P**roposition. How do you stand out above your competition? Why should your prospects do business with you versus any of the other businesses?

Unique Selling Proposition means the factor or consideration presented by a seller as the reason that one company, product or service is different from and better than that of the competition.

So to start, create one (USP) and put it everywhere. Put it on your Website, Business Cards, Bids, Proposals, follow up messages, Ads, etc! Any and ALL Marketing Materials should contain your USP.

Later on, you can have more than one USP. Perhaps one for service, and another for products. Or even different ones for different services and for different products.

How to Create a USP

One Simple Method:

1. End Result Prospect Wants.

2. Include specific time frame.

3. Address any objections.

This is our USP to give you a sample:

MarketingBlueprintForContactors.com helps contractors DOUBLE their Profits in 90 Days or LESS!

Let's see if this fits into this simple method:

1. End Result Prospect Wants.
   Double Your Profits

2. Include specific time frame.
   in 90 Days or Less

3. Address any objections.
   Comment here. I use to Say "Guarantee" however for money or profit related items, that can be a "Red Flag" so I stopped using it.

Another Sample: "We warrant all our products 10 years! Not 2 years or less like others."

Example 1: Fresh, hot pizza delivered in 30 minutes or less, guaranteed.

Who is this?

Domino's Pizza!

Most people don't know the story behind Domino's Pizza. Their USP made them who they became!

The story starts with two young men determined to run a small business to pay for college. The pizza shop was not as successful as expected and one guy decided to bail out. Tom Monaghan kept the business going and survived ONLY after he came up with the legendary USP!

Tony Bernard

"Fresh, hot pizza delivered in 30 minutes or less, guaranteed"

Ten words that changed his life!

Ten words that changed the pizza industry!

It was a brilliant USP. It included two product benefits a specific time frame, plus a guarantee!

Fresh and Hot – Two Product benefits

30 Minutes – Specific time frame (not quick, not soon, but 30 minutes)

PLUS a Guarantee!

Very well done!

Notice that there is no mention about:

- highest quality
     Or
- best price

That is not what they were striving for.

Because of this USP the company added on average, 3 new franchises each week in the 1980's. (Estimated 7,500 global locations).

In 1998 Tom sold his business for an estimated $1 billion.

Think about this! What really made Domino's Pizza? The USP is the main thing! That is a great example of the leverage of marketing!

Example 2: 15 minutes could save you 15% or more on car Insurance.

Who is this?

Geico!

Again, our USP is

MarketingBlueprintForContactors.com helps contractors DOUBLE their Profits in 90 Days or LESS!

We can say this because we use our Proven Propriety Marketing System.

Now it is time to start creating your own USP!

You have a simple method and some samples right here so no better time than right now to start it!

Remember, One Simple Method:

1. End Result Prospect Wants.

2. Include specific time frame.

3. Address any objections.

Step 1 - End Result Your Prospect Wants:

_____

_____

_____

Step 2 - Include specific time frame:

_____

_____

_____

Step 3 - Address any objections

_____

_____

_____

Final Steps:

A. Write out a draft USP here. You have to start somewhere.

_____

_____

_____

B. Review the above USP and think about it, but say it differently this time (More concise).

_____

_____

_____

C. Review the two USPs above and try writing it one more time, slightly different and even more concise!

_____

_____

_____

Okay, between the different versions above you should now have one that will work excellent for you. **Start using it right away! If you need more space, take all you need. BUT do this NOW!**

NOTE: Your USP should make you feel uncomfortable. You may be concerned that people will take advantage of you. You need to be very specific about it and make sure you are not giving away the farm. However, if crafted properly, it will get you far more new sales than what some might take advantage of you. **Again, don't give away the farm and test it. Do small test to see how much it helps. Then once you see how well it helps gain additional business, you can roll it out.**

This book is based on the Video Presentation at

MarketingBlueprintForContractorsBook.com/Presentation

The presentation is updated from time to time because we want to provide you the latest information.

Chapter 7

Profit Multiplier 3

Follow Up

"Don't use big words, they mean so little."

Oscar Wilde

Do you currently Follow Up on all your prospects, proposals or bids?

Be honest.

Do you ALWAYS follow up on your prospects, proposals or bids?

This is a yes or no answer!

You need to ALWAYS follow up and having it automated is key. That way, if someone is out of the office on vacation or out sick, the follow up will still automatically work for you, bring you in new clients like clockwork!

Sometimes following up doesn't cut it. It is ALWAYS or NOT!

Follow up is continuing to educate prospect and or clients about why you are the only Contractor to pick. It's best done by providing additional value or education.

Remember, you are different and your USP should clearly state that and you can remind them in your follow up messaging!

Question for you. What percent of companies or sales people never Follow Up? Take a guess. 28, 38, 48, 58, or 68%?

And the answer is …

48% of the time there is NO Follow up by either the company or sales person. With today's technology, that is a sin.

25% of the time there's 1 Follow up.

12% of the time there's 2 Follow ups.

10% of the time there's 3 Follow ups.

5% of the time there's 4 or more Follow ups.

This is good information to know and you can see it graphically below.

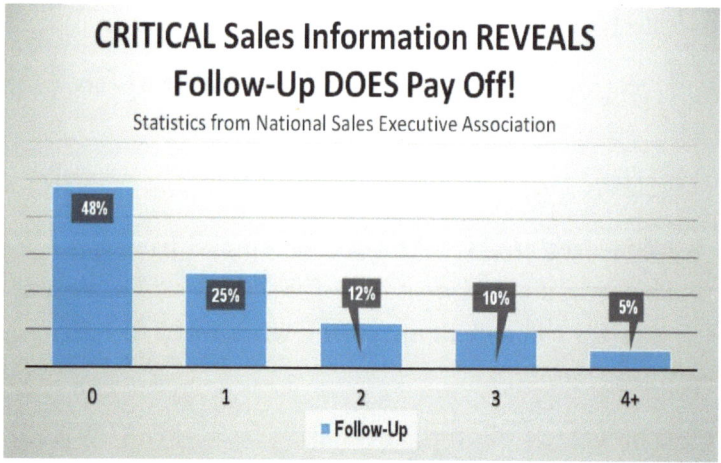

Now let's compare that information to when sales actually happen.

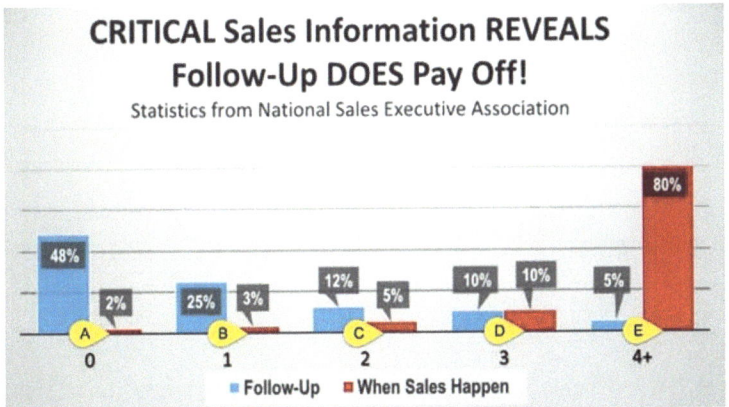

As the percentage of follow up declines (blue bars on the left), the percentage of sales increases (red bars on the right)!

Point A – 48% of the time NO Follow up, yet 2% of sales happen there.

Point B – 25% of the time 1 Follow up, with 3% of sales happen there.

Point C – 12% of the time 2 Follow ups, with 5% of sales happen there.

Point D – 10% of the time 3 Follow ups, with 10% of sales happen there.

Point E – 5% of the time 4 or more Follow ups, with 80% of sales happening!

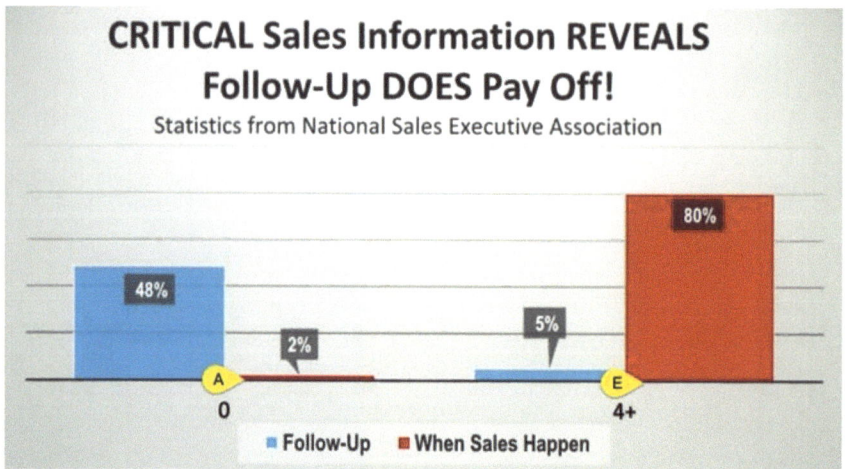

This is HUGE!!!

Okay, so look at Point A to Point E again! **That is a difference of 40 times.** Now I'm not saying if you implement a follow up system your sales will increase 40 times. I know you would agree that some improvements would happen! Pick a number. 10%, 20%, perhaps even more?

Even if you have a follow up system in place now, by changing your approach (educational based follow up information), you can significantly increase your sales or profits!

Keep in mind that follow up is not calling and asking for the sale. It is continuing to educate the prospect why you are the contractor of choice and provide more educational information about the product or service they asked about! Don't forget to keep your USP in front of them all the time. Business cards, follow-up messaging, bid, proposal and any other marketing or ad materials!

The use of different modalities of delivery of your follow up messages to your prospect will greatly increase your results. Examples being: the use of texting, Voice Mail, Email and Video greatly help improves the results of Follow-Up!

Tony Bernard

NOTE: Contact us to learn about what tool would be best for your specific situation and your objectives.

Tony@MarketingBlueprintForContractorsBook.com

This book is based on the Video Presentation at

MarketingBlueprintForContractorsBook.com/Presentation

The presentation is updated from time to time because we want to provide you the latest information.

CHAPTER 8

PROFIT MULTIPLIER 4

STRATEGIC MESSAGING FORMULA (SMF)

"On average, 8 out of 10 people
will read your headline copy,
but only 2 out of 10 will read the rest"

Brian Clark, Copyblogger

How to write an Ad

The old "AIDA" Formula works well, masterminded by a gentleman by the name of Elias St. Elmo Lewis (American advertising advocate) in 1898.

AIDA is an acronym used in marketing to describe a list of items that were essential to ad writing.

A – Attention
I – Interest
D – Desire
A – Action (Call to Action)

A – Attention: attract the attention of the customer. Stand out, make them take notice.

I – Interest: raise customer interest by demonstrating advantages, and benefits.

D – Desire: convince prospects/customers/clients that they want and desire the product or service and that it will satisfy all their needs.

A – Action: lead customers towards taking immediate action.

Many companies still use this method.

However ….. 1898 was a long time ago. The psychology of selling has NOT changed, however improvements have been made in the methods!

What if I could show you a Proven Proprietary way to predict the likelihood of success for your ad or marketing materials?!

Would you want it?

Introducing the **Strategic Messaging Formula**

This formula has been put together from years of combined efforts and a proven system that will enhance your marketing message plus provide an indication of the likelihood of the success of your ad or marketing materials.

The **Strategic Messaging Formula** will grab your prospect's attention, will tell them how you can solve their problem, why they should trust you, and why they should choose to do business with you over and above any and all other choices they have. Don't you want to be able to use a tool like this? Can you see the power of this?

Your marketing message should "speak" to your prospect. This is done by appealing to your prospect's "hot buttons" or those words that trigger an emotional reaction.

The following is a simplified five-step method for creating your marketing message with our **Proven Proprietary System.**

1. Capture – Headline

2. Connect – Sub-Headline

3. Inform – Body Copy

4. Incentivize – Call to Action

5. Format - Overall layout, fonts, flow, all work together.

Okay, let's get more into the details ...

1. **Capture:** This is the job of the **Headline!** Grab the attention of your intended person.

2. **Connect:** This is the job of the **Sub-Headline.** Keep the attention of the intended person on a more emotional level.

3. **Inform:** This is the job of the **body copy**, the main section of the piece. This should educate and build **Your case** as to why **You** are the **contractor of choice! Include your USP.**

4. **Incentivize:** Lower the risk barrier, make an Irresistible offer, Guarantee, Free Report, etc. Must provide a specific **call to action as well. ALWAYS Only ask for ONE call to action.**

5. **Format:** The layout, flow, fonts all play a vital role in the success of the ad.

Here is the general layout of the Proven Layout that WORKS!

HOT BUTTON LOADED HEADLINE

that Captures Attention Goes Here

Subheadline Goes Here. Remember to use activators that are important and relevant

Subheadline that Promises to Inform the Prospect Goes Here.

This is where the informational body content goes. This content should build your case like an attorney does. Use as much specific information and as much detailed evidence as possible. Don't stress out too much over the text here since the headlines and incentive will do most of the work. Short paragraphs that are about this long work well.

Subheadline that Continues to Hit Hot Buttons Goes Here

Remember to use the writing guidelines when you write the body copy. In short, always write like people talk. Your grade does not come from a teacher, but from the marketplace. The only thing that matters is what works—not true grammar. Also, don't try to be cute and especially don't try to be an english professor.

FREE SOMETHING!

Put an image or description of whatever the incentive is to take the next step in the buying process. Then make sure the instructions to take the next step are obvious.

visit: YourWebsite.com

Logo goes above. Other contact information or necessary information can go here (phone number, address, etc.)

That is the general layout, now let me show you each specific element.

You can clearly see the format above, now let me show you the grading system to help ensure the likelihood for a successful ad or marketing materials.

The following is the Summary Evaluation form, showing just the 5 Critical Elements, and the bottom contains the overall rating. **Note that most ads and marketing materials are 2 on a scale of 0 to 10. That is pitiful and their results reflect this poor ad!**

StrategicMessageFormula.com
Summary Evaluation
Use this worksheet to grade any marketing piece.
Total Average Grade 6 or higher will work, however the higher the better.

1 - Capture: Attention of Intended Prospect: (Headline)

2 - Connect: Emotionally Keep Attention, Provide more Information (Sub-Headline)

3 - Inform: Educate and Building Your Case (Body Copy, etc.)

4 - Incentivize: Lower Risk and or Irresistible Offer, Guarantee (Call to Action)

5 - Format: Flow, Fonts, Follow-Up

Total Number Of Points: _____ Divided By 5 = _____ This Is Your Marketing Piece Evaluation Score (See Comments below)

What The Average Score Means:
- ☐ S-0: **Total waste of your money.**
- ☐ S-2: Poor Ad with Platitudes, will **get average results.** Most ads are S-2.
- ☐ S-4: Captures attention; will **get OK Results.**
- ☐ S-6: Captures and Connects, lacks power. **Good Results Likely.**
- ☐ S-8: Captures and Connects, Powerful ad. **Great Results Likely.**
- ☐ S-10: Ranks well in all area and **Tremendous Results Expected.**

StrategicMessageFormula.com

The Detailed Evaluation form is proprietary information, so I'm not able to show the details of the evaluation form.

However, what we do is grade each element on a scale of 0 to 10, and then total the score for each of the 5 Critical Elements. Take that total score and divide by 5 to get the average grade and that tells us the likelihood of the success of that ad or marketing material!

Remember that most ads and marketing materials are 2. 2 out of 10 that is! What if your child or grandchild came home with a 20 (out of 100) on their quiz, test or report card, what would you do?

I know I would want to get them some help to improve this poor grade.

Yet most businesses accept this poor level of performance for their hard earned money by not using a Proven way to create ads or marketing materials.

You work hard enough for your money, don't you want to optimize the money you invest in ads and marketing materials?

It is not your fault. You just need someone that is looking out for your interest, not to sell you the product or service that they sell.

This is a limited time offer and it is on a first come, first served basis. There is no way to know how long I can make this offer, so submit your ad ASAP and hopefully I can review your ad for the limited time offer of ONLY $20!*

Email us at:
Support@CornerstoneMarketingCompany.com
Subject: $20 Book Bonus Ad Review (Limited Time)*
 Need to verify that we have time to do this for you.

I'm confident that we can double your response rate on just about any ad. Email us NOW to get your current ad score!

 * price may be subject to change.

StrategicMessageFormula.com
Detailed Evaluation Worksheet

Use this worksheet to grade any marketing piece.
Total Average Grade 6 or higher will work, however the higher the better.

---

1 - Capture: Attention of Intended Prospect: (Headline)

Points

- 0   No headline at all
- 2   Company name or logo used as headline. Nothing to cause reader to continue to pay attention
- 4   *(illegible)*
- 6   *(illegible)*
- 8   *(illegible)*
- 10 *(illegible)*

_____

2 - Connect: Emotionally Keep Attention, Provide more Information (Sub-Headline)

Points

- 0   If headline score is P-0, P-1, or P-2 ...then automatic score of P-0 here
- 2   No subheadline or anything else to cause the reader to emotionally connect
- 4   *(illegible)*
- 6   *(illegible)*
- 8   *(illegible)*
- 10 *(illegible)*

_____

3 - Inform: Educate and Building Your Case (Body Copy, etc.)

Points

- 0   No information presented that builds any case. Typical "creative" or "entertainment" based copy used (institutional)
- 2   Lists or bullet points of common and/or obvious information listed
- 4   *(illegible)*
- 6   *(illegible)*
- 8   *(illegible)*
- 10 *(illegible)*

_____

4 - Incentivize: Lower Risk and or Irresistible Offer, Guarantee (Call to Action)

Points

- 0   No incentive available or offer presented
- 2   Contact information only is listed (phone number, website, address, etc.)
- 4   *(illegible)*
- 6   *(illegible)*
- 8   *(illegible)*
- 10 *(illegible)*

_____

5 - Format: Flow, Fonts, Follow-Up

Points

- 0   A total mess, try again
- 2   Does not flow, no logical reason for any placements, haphazardly done, not professional
- 4   *(illegible)*
- 6   *(illegible)*
- 8   *(illegible)*
- 10 *(illegible)*

_____

Total Number Of Points: _____ **Divided By 5 =** _____ This is Your Marketing Piece Evaluation Score (See Comments below)

What The Average Score Means:

- S-0:   Total waste of your money.
- S-2:   Poor Ad with Platitudes, will get average results. Most ads are S-2.
- S-4:   Captures attention; will get OK Results.
- S-6:   Captures and Connects, lacks power. **Good Results Likely.**
- S-8:   Captures and Connects, Powerful ad. **Great Results Likely.**
- S-10: Ranks well in all area and **Tremendous Results Expected.**

StrategicMessageFormula.com

Most ads' grade is 2. Remember, that is on a scale up to 10. So that is a score of about 20% (out of 100%). WOW! Why Accept this poor performance for your hard earned money! You deserve more for your hard earned money and we can help!

So, let's recap the power of this Proven Proprietary System called the Strategic Messaging Formula!

We take any ad or marketing material, and grade it based on the 5 Proven Critical Elements. Once we have the starting grade of the original ad or marketing material, we can work on the weak elements to improve the quality of them to increase your overall Success rate!

The Proprietary details on the form tell us exactly what Critical Elements to work on to improve the likelihood of making the ad or marketing materials much more successful!

No guess work, when we use our proven proprietary system!

In the case studies you'll have access to on-line, we will show you the grades of the original ad compared that to the revised ad.

In Case Study 1, the original ad was graded at a 2 and the revised ad after using the Strategic Messaging Formula, became a 9.2.

That is a huge improvement, however what is even better, is the performance of the actual ad!

Click here to see the actual display ads and the details! **This will be eye-opening!**

MarketingBlueprintForContractors.com/CaseStudy

MESSAGING Matters!

To further show that messaging is CRITICAL and how words matter, click this link to watch a great short 2 minute video.

http://www.youtube.com/watch?v=Hzgzim5m7oU

The **Messag**e and **words** in the above video show the great importance they both have!!

With our Proven Proprietary System, the **"Strategic Messaging Formula"** you will see a dramatic improvement in your ad or marketing materials and **I guarantee that!!**

This formula, works on ALL ads and Marketing Materials!

Before you pay for a POOR Performing Display Ad (yellow page, newspaper, trade journal, etc), submit it to us to see the likelihood of its success!

Check out Chapter 15 – Bonus 3 for a limited time offer to possibly have your ad graded! There is a small charge to eliminate the tire kickers!

This book is based on the Video Presentation at

MarketingBlueprintForContractorsBook.com/Presentation

The presentation is updated from time to time because we want to provide you the latest information.

CHAPTER 9

PROFIT MULTIPLIER 5

FREQUENTLY ASKED QUESTIONS (FAQ)

"You can't push your sales messages on your fans too often."

Andrea Vahl

Frequently Asked Questions (FAQs)

You know about these. The typical questions that you get about your product or service. You can start with just 5 to 10 items. You can always add more or change them.

This not only gives you a slight edge over others, it will save you time not answering these same questions time and time again. **Plus, you can craft a great answer and this will ensure that the same compelling answer is always used!**

Read that last sentence again and let that sink in!

Written format FAQ - I want you to have them in written format for your website, proposals, bids, etc.

Video format FAQ - I want you to also have them in video format for your website and a DVD for your proposals or bid. Video format could be you directly on camera (your face on camera) or just you using PowerPoint or some other presentation tool and recording you reading the presentation or a script.

A small portion of websites do have these: I would estimate about 11%. But if you include these with your proposals or bids, that will help set you apart.

This book is based on the Video Presentation at

MarketingBlueprintForContractorsBook.com/Presentation

The presentation is updated from time to time because we want to provide you the latest information.

CHAPTER 10

PROFIT MULTIPLIER 6

SHOULD ASKED QUESTIONS (SAQ)

"Make the prospect a more informed buyer with content"

Robert Simon, Four Season Hotels

Should Ask Questions (SAQs)

This will **REALLY** set you apart! It also takes a shift of thinking to create them.

If you had a friend or relative needing your product or services that lived 4 states away. What would you want them to ask their local Contractor to know that they are picking the right Contractor? What are the inside questions that should be asked? Remember, you already have the FAQs done. The SAQs are the deeper level questions.

This is where you REALLY set yourself apart from other contractors by providing your prospects with the Should Ask Questions of any contractor they would hire to do work for them!

Here are some samples that could be used, adapted or adopted.

SAQ1 – What insurances are carried? Proof needs to be provided and also ensure they are current and not expiring in the middle of your project or job.

Note: You are looking for General Liability and Worker's Compensation. If they will have any subcontractors on the job, they must also provide the same proof.

What many homeowners don't realize is that if a contractor does not have worker's compensation, and an employee gets injured while working on your home, then the homeowner's insurance policy may be the one that has to cover the cost of the injury.

SAQ2 – Provide a time-line for the work, also known as a schedule. The level of detail depends on complexity of the job and any other interactions they may have to have with you or other contractors. This could open up a lengthy discussion, beyond the scope of this book.

SAQ3 – What is your warranty or guarantee? Keep in mind that labor and materials both have to be addressed. You should include something about a guarantee in your USP. That way it is right out in front of your prospect and should set you apart, if it is a great warranty or guarantee.

SAQ4 – Will you have any subcontractors and if so, provide a list and they will also have to meet all the requirements that you have provided to me.

LAST SAQ – Can you include all of these details in writing on the proposal? Oral agreements are agreements, but you know you want everything in writing! Make sure the details are included. Not just some high level summary statement that has no specifics included.

I'm sure you **CAN SEE the VALUE IN THIS!**

Written format SAQ - I want you to have them in written format for your website, proposals, bids, etc.

Video format SAQ - I want you to also have them in video format for your website and a DVD for your proposals or bids. Video format could be you directly on camera (your face on camera) or just you using PowerPoint or some other presentation tool and recording you reading the presentation or a script.

If you look out on the web, there is hardly anyone including SAQs. Here is your chance to set yourself apart!

This book is based on the Video Presentation at

MarketingBlueprintForContractorsBook.com/Presentation

The presentation is updated from time to time because we want to provide you the latest information.

CHAPTER 11

LET'S RE-CAP

"What you prefer or what your designer prefers doesn't matter if it's not getting you conversion."

Naomi Niles

You Don't Have To Do It Alone

In Fact, Doing It Alone Is **Your** Choice Just Like Not Doing It Alone Is A Choice. **Click here to Apply** for the Free Consultation to get your questions answered.

MarketingBlueprintForContractors.com/Consultation

I'm also reminded of ....

JOHN RUSKIN QUOTE: *"It's unwise to pay too much, but it's worse to pay too little. When you pay too much, you lose a little money—that is all. When you pay too little, you sometimes lose everything, because the thing you bought was incapable of doing the thing it was bought to do. The common law of business balance prohibits paying a little and getting a lot—it can't be done. If you deal with the lowest bidder, it is well to add something for the risk you run, and if you do that you will have enough to pay for something better."*

You may be wondering why I'm giving all this great information!

Actually two reasons:

1. Because I Love Helping People!

2. It's how I attract, great new clients – Action taking, open minded clients that is!

I'm sure you are finding this information eye opening! That's great! I love to help people that want help and are action takers! **So, click here to apply** for the free consultation to see **if you qualify.**

MarketingBlueprintForContractors.com/Consultation

I heard this years ago and it is so true.

"Doing what you have always done, will get you what you have always gotten. NOW is the time for change!"

I want to acknowledge YOUR time investment in reading this book! Congratulate yourself! Over 90% of people would not have read to this point and they wonder why things are not improving in their lives or business! **See you are an action taker! Excellent!**

This Information comes from years of study, research and hundreds of Actual Case Studies!

Summary of the 6 Profit Multipliers!

Tony Bernard

Six Profit Multipliers To
Double YOUR PROFITS
In 90 Days or LESS!

1. **Marketing Mindset**
   a. *Fragmented Marketing*
      No Consistent messaging or Strategy across all channels.

   b. *Use of Platitudes*
      Words & phrases that are devoid of any real meaning.

   c. *Type of Marketing Used*
      Use Direct Response, with one specific call to action.

2. **Unique Selling Proposition (USP)**
   Why should someone do business with you verses another company?

3. **Follow Up**
   48% of the time there is NO Follow up! Use some automated method or system to ensure proper follow up is always done!

4. **Strategic Messaging Formula (SMF)**
   a. Capture – Headlines job
   b. Connect – Sub-Headlines job
   c. Inform – Body copy
   d. Incentivize – Call to action
   e. Format – Flow, layout, fonts, etc

5. **Frequently Asked Questions (FAQ)**
   Typically asked questions answered

6. **Should Ask Questions (SAQ)**
   What are the inside questions that should be asked.

MarketingBlueprintForContractors.com

It cost me over $140,670 and more than 24 years to learn what you have learned in this short and concise book.

Your Marketing **will become a Predictable System once you start implementing any of these 6 Profit Multipliers!**

This book is based on the Video Presentation at

MarketingBlueprintForContractorsBook.com/Presentation

The presentation is updated from time to time because we want to provide you the latest information.

CHAPTER 12

CASE STUDIES

"The difference between a successful person and others is not a lack of strength, not a lack of knowledge, but rather a lack of will."

Vince Lombardi

The main point is that the "Strategic Messaging Formula" works on ALL ads and marketing materials!

Here is a link to a video showing the two case studies. One is a Moving Company and the second is a Roofing Company.

MarketingBlueprintForContractors.com/CaseStudy

You will see the original ad and the revised ad using the **"Strategic Messaging Formula."** Also included is the ranking of each ad (Original and the Revised). **This is eye opening and will show you the POWER in this Formula!**

One Case study got a 267% increase in response and the other one got 1,367%!

Just imagine, getting 100% increase in your ads from just this one pillar. Then add the other pillars on top! Can you see how Fast and Easy it is to **Double YOUR Profits in 90 days or LESS!?**

That is, when you use proven strategies!

MarketingBlueprintForContractors.com/CaseStudy

MarketingBlueprintForContractors.com

While These RESULTS are NOT TYPICAL, when you use a **Proven Formula**, the likelihood **of Success GREATLY Increases!**

Whether you are a General Contractor or Specialty Contractor, the information contained in the **Strategic Messaging Formula** and this book **WILL change your business forever!** Of course, you will have to implement any one or combination of these strategies!

I hope you took notes and will apply some if not all of these valuable Pillars, tips or strategies!

Don't forget to apply for your FREE 30 Minute Consultation!

FREE CONSULTATION, If you qualify!

MarketingBlueprintForContractors.com/Consultation

This book is based on the Video Presentation at

MarketingBlueprintForContractorsBook.com/Presentation

The presentation is updated from time to time because we want to provide you the latest information.

CHAPTER 13

BONUS #1

FREE CONSULTATION

>>> *IF YOU QUALIFY* <<<

"The best marketing doesn't feel like marketing."

Tom Fishburne, Marketoonist

To help you even more, I'll work with you to help answer any questions you have and develop a **Personalized Marketing Plan, if you qualify.**

My time is very limited, so **book a time right now. It needs to be a good fit. Life is too short to not have a great time while helping others Double their profits!**

You see the link or button below, go there **NOW** before my schedule becomes full and all time slots are taken!

"Doing what you have always done in Marketing, will get you what you have always gotten! NOW is the time to DOUBLE Your Profits!"

Schedule your 30 minute, no obligation Marketing Consultation NOW to get YOUR Questions Answered!

MarketingBlueprintForContractors.com/Consultation

CHAPTER 14

BONUS #2

GOOGLE MY BUSINESS

"Too often, feeling intimidated becomes our excuse not to be awesome."

Scott Stratten

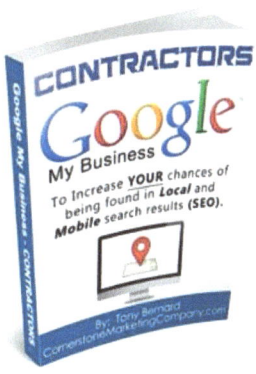

What Is Google My Business?

Google My Business is an invaluable tool for any contractor. Understanding the fundamentals of this platform will increase your chances of being found in *local* and *mobile* search results.

As a small business looking to connect with more local consumers, *these* search results are the most valuable ones you can pursue. Getting ranked locally is also a lot easier and less time consuming than attempting to compete with the entire world. Not only that, but focusing on local rankings will also help you reach geo-targeted consumers (local) who are more likely to become real customers.

To get this report, FREE, click here!

MarketingBlueprintForContractors.com/GoogleMyBusiness

Un-Announced BOOK Bonus! By Purchasing this book, you are gifted an **Additional 25% discount** off the already discounted offer for "Google My Business". **This is a service that we may stop at any time, due to the demands of our time with our clients.**

To get this discount you will have to tell us about it this additional discount contained in this book when you order this service from us.

This book is based on the Video Presentation at

MarketingBlueprintForContractorsBook.com/Presentation

The presentation is updated from time to time because we want to provide you the latest information.

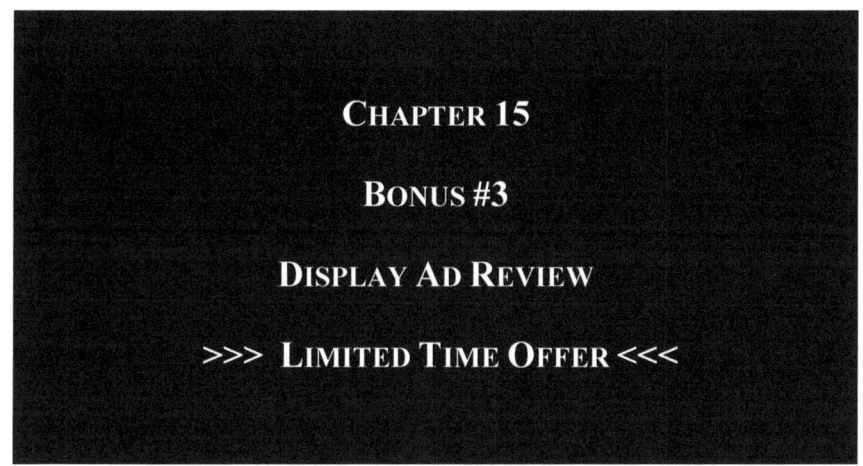

CHAPTER 15

BONUS #3

DISPLAY AD REVIEW

>>> LIMITED TIME OFFER <<<

"Start testing and stop arguing."

John Correll

Most display ads score about a 2 out of 10 (or 20%). What if your child or grandchild came home with a 20 (out of 100) on a test? Would you want them to do something about it?

So, why accept this poor level of ad performance when we can fix it for you! I'm confident that we can double your ad response rate. Same ad cost, however twice the response rate!

What are you waiting for? Let us review one of your ads and help you right NOW!

By waiting you are leaving money on the table.

Don't you want to know your scores before you invest in your next ad?

So, before you submit your next display ad (Yellow Pages, newspaper, trade journal, etc), **have us review your ad for ONLY**

$20*. I'm charging this small fee to eliminate the wasteful tire kickers that will just get something because it is free!

This is a limited time offer and it is on a first come, first served basis. There is no way to know how long I can make this offer, so submit your ad ASAP and hopefully I can review your ad for the limited time offer of ONLY $20*!

Email us at:

Support@CornerstoneMarketingCompany.com

Subject: $20* Book Bonus Ad Review (Limited Time)

I'm confident that we can double your response rate on just about any ad. Email us NOW to get your current ad score!

* Price may be subject to change.

This book is based on the Video Presentation at

MarketingBlueprintForContractorsBook.com/Presentation

The presentation is updated from time to time because we want to provide you the latest information.

Tony Bernard

ABOUT THE AUTHOR

"Doing what you have always done
in Marketing,
will get you what you have always gotten!
NOW is the time to DOUBLE YOUR Profits!"

Tony Bernard

Tony Bernard, is an Amazon #1 International Best Selling Author, Speaker, International Consultant and CEO of Cornerstone Marketing Company (**CornerstoneMarketingCompany.com**) and Founder of Blueprint For Successful Projects (**BluePrintForSuccessfulProjects.com**) and author and creator of Marketing Blueprint For Contractors (**MarketingBlueprintForContractors.com**).

This is Tony's first book and using a specific strategy, he was able to become an Amazon #1 Best Seller Author in a relatively short period of time compared to what most people think. This might be one strategy that he recommends to be used in your business during the Free 30 minute consultation if you qualify.

He started private consulting back in 1991 including international assignments while working primarily in the Construction

Industry. For the past 35 years, he has had the good fortune to work on over $15 Billion Dollars' worth of projects so far.

Started in Marketing in 1986 as a franchise owner of the Success Motivation Institute (SMI), and studied with great mentors to hone his skills, including Jay Abraham, Dan Kennedy, Frank Kern, Brendon Burchard, Jimmy Harding, and Corey Rudl to name a few.

Results-based approach has given Tony a unique perspective and has given him the undeniable reputation for being known for getting results and exceeding expectations and having a core mission to deliver exceptional value to his clients' time and time again.

 Combining his international consulting experience made becoming a Certified "Power Marketing Consultant" the perfect addition to round out Tony's skills set and bring about the ultimate combination of systems, tools, and marketing psychology for today's changing business climate.

"The use of our **Strategic Messaging Formula'** *virtually guarantees your company will double profits in 90 Days or LESS, PLUS dominate your local industry in less than a year because it is based on our Proven Proprietary Marketing System."*

"Success can be achieved by three major factors: 1) Asking better quality questions, 2) Adopting & adapting best practices from other companies and industries and 3) Proper implementation. Remember, Doing what you have always done, will get you what you have always gotten. NOW is the time for change!" Says Tony Bernard.

This book is based on the Video Presentation at

MarketingBlueprintForContractorsBook.com/Presentation

The presentation is updated from time to time because we want to provide you the latest information.

SUMMARY OF WEB LINKS

Follow Up System
    Contact us for current recommendations.

Free 30 Minute Consultation (If qualified)

MarketingBlueprintForContractors.com/Consultation

Strategic Messaging Formula

StrategicMessagingFormula.com

Case Studies

MarketingBlueprintForContractors.com/CaseStudy

The Power of Messaging and Words

www.youtube.com/watch?v=Hzgzim5m7oU

Contractor – Google My Business

MarketingBlueprintForContractors.com/GoogleMyBusiness

Display Ad Review (Limited Time)
    Email us at:
        Support@MarketingBlueprintForContractors.com
        Subject: **$20 Book Bonus Ad Review (Limited Time)**

    Need to verify we have time to do this and current pricing.

This book is based on the Video Presentation at

MarketingBlueprintForContractorsBook.com/Presentation

The presentation is updated from time to time because we want to provide you the latest information.